When my body has withered
and I am once again returned to the earth,
all that will remain is my writing

FRANCES IVY

Dear Moon

2017

Undo my hair
then
let me rest
Leave the window
half-open,
please
Then go
I have been brave
for so very long
but now
I will crumble
just for a little
while

The sun is slowly returning,
birds sit waiting in the trees
Two weeks ago the sky opened up
and rain poured over our city,
unforgivingly
Everybody took shelter,
in their lovers embrace
or under the wings of their protectors
I, however, stood soaking wet in the street,
still like a marble statue
For I have nowhere to go
anymore,
I'm not safe anywhere

Dip your fingers
in the softness of
my sorrows
Can you feel it,
the depth that
embrace you
so easily,
urging you to dive
deep into it,
find its essence
In the beginning
you'll feel as if
you're sliding down
a gentle waterfall
touched by kind hands,
but eventually it'll get
darker, muddy and cold
and you'll wish
that you never touched me
to begin with

Paper thin
The fragility of my mind
will destroy me
How an empty word
thrown in anger
can cut me so deeply,
shatter me –
like a glass vase

Talk to me
as if you talked to the night sky,
the way you utter a longing
or a prayer in your loneliest hour
Tell me everything you wish you'd told your father
or lover or friend,
and I will listen to every single word
that floats from the abyss that's within you –
because I understand

I can not be the shallow shell of a waste basket
who will talk to you about things
that does not matter anymore,
for I don't care
about things without meaning,
or people without depth

Small ray of sunlight
basking in the glory of her God
The air chilled as if occupied by restless ghosts,
winter still lingering,
invisibly
She lay among daffodils,
shivering in the arms of her lover
Seen but not really seen
Transparent, dust spread out over the sea,
tears of a child unwanted
Desired,
but never loved

The starless night sky above me,
so silent and so widely open,
watching me like a protective father
My fingers bleeding
from desperately trying to peel off all the layers,
in search of my soul
I question sometimes
whether or not there is a real me,
for until now,
I have been so many people

I admit that we ruined each other,
every morning as the light reflected upon our sins
we died over and over again
In the end of it all I walked away
like he was nothing,
left him
covered in smoky ash after burning him to the bones
I laughed as the sun rose,
because of how stupid he could be –
thinking that he would be the one hurting me

Mountains falling asleep
Trees hugging themselves in the sullen shadows
Deer laying down to rest in the grass
A cold mist seem to rise out of nothing,
licking my limbs,
travelling past me like hissing voices –
a cornered snake in distress

Dear moon, mother,
so far you've never lied to me,
but will I run
forever

The sun has set,
the landscape turned colorless,
old wounds opening up like flowers

What a perfect moment to disappear

Fly away little crow
Deep, deep into the blackness of the wild woods
Back where you belong
You'll find salvation among the branches
and peace will again enter your drained soul
Your tired wings will also regain their strength
and you'll be warm for winter
So fly away little crow
Back to where you're happy

Why are you hiding
inside my head
There must be other places
to pester

My body felt weightless
as a piece of abandoned paper
Floating face up towards velvet skies in the river of ease
The night was chilly
but I was wrapped in thick black feathers
stolen from a beautiful swan dying in the sands
I stayed with it for a moment before the current caught me
I sensed plenty of suffering and sorrow
Poor animal with a soul much like mine
We might have been twins in our past lives
and maybe we were
in this one too
I rocked back and forth with the motion of the water
Counted stars
Searched for images among them
I questioned if earth could really be the only planet
which carry life
What terrible misary
and what a disappointment
to all the Gods and angels that we've failed
As silky clouds abruptly invaded my vision
the landscape turned somber and faint
Like I had entered a parallel universe
where time passed twice as slow
A temporary illusion
Welcomed

He said he'd write a novel,
for every time I thought
the world
would come to an end
So that when I finally realized
how my life was infinite,
there would be enough stories
to always remind me of the magic,
that undoubtly surrounds us

Pretty as a pale rose,
she whirls among nightshade in the back of the garden,
effortlessly
The moon smiles as the girl dances,
slowly around and around
Her eyes closed, a faint smile on her peachy lips,
completely mesmerized by the darkness –
where she feels safe

Hold me until I heal
Lift my spirit
out of the gutter
I'm stuck
Let your breath
breathe life into me
For I'm a dying fire
and you're my air

You are made of
the most delicate fabric,
stitched with brittle thread
You bend and you break
by the hands of those
who have no respect for
what wasn't theirs to use
in the first place

Yes I may be quiet,
sometimes
I may even be a little
strange
But you don't have to be
loud, or hide
your truth
behind polished walls
to deserve being heard,
or noticed

He loved me once, I'm sure he did
I was never his first priority,
but he must have loved me
Dark velvet curtains, crisp bed sheets,
his smile was really beautiful for a man –
it always surprised me
I think he missed me during the day, or maybe he didn't
Honestly I never cared about the truth
It was never important to me
I only cared about that exact moment,
because in that moment I was his,
and nothing else existed

I've seen how you change
the ones around you,
what beautiful power you possess

Do not let it go to waste

Shelter me
From the worries
of the world
Let me sleep in the depths
of your shallows
In a crystal chrysalis
lay curled

As evening falls around us,
so does our love
A breath of wind seeps through the leaves
and shakes the ground on which he walks heavily,
dragging his feet in the muddy water
The two of us,
short-lived as the fragile life of a dragonfly
Behind us willows weep quietly,
for how could they not
You smell like the rain, he says –
All dirty and sad
I smile at him,
for underneath that damp coat of gloomy thunder
he's still my heart and my soul,
but unable to see that I'm hurting
too

I let my nightgown fall to the floor
My skin is sore,
covered in rosy marks,
dirty fingerprints
I step into the bath,
the warm water
is filled with soft bubbles that soothes me
It makes me feel safe,
so I just lay there
and let life wash away
for a moment

At night my bed
turns into an ocean
Usually still and peaceful,
wavering cotton waves
rocking me gently
In it my body
looks tiny
floating on endless
threads of silk

But now as I lay down
I feel the anguish
Being tossed around by
infinite forces
that could suck me under
in the blink of an eye
I'm often strong enough
to fight
but tonight I'm too tired –
so I will let it have me

We hide under heavy cloaks
Behind stale faced masks
Have you forgotten
what's underneath –
Who you actually are
Maybe it's time to rediscover
the softness
within you

Take it off

A feathery blanket lay over the garden
Once again winter is here
I saw the birds take off a few weeks ago
and remember wishing that they stayed
Please don't go,
it'll be gone in no time anyway
The window sill which I lean on is cold,
making my skin tickle
Damn you world
for covering up the ugliness that surrounds us
It should be thrown in our face
But nature is good in that way,
always quick to heal every gushing wound
so that we can forget,
go back to oblivion
Although the truth is that as our own egos get fuller,
wider, bigger – stuffed with materialistic fulfillment –
humanity becomes emptier

How can we be expected
to feel beautiful
when we are constantly told
we are not

There are some,
who will discard you
when they can no longer use you
to move forward
There are some,
who will make up lies
and twist the reality
for you to look bad,
in order to feel better about themselves
There are some whom you love,
who will step over you
regardless

Let them go

He takes my hand,
his breath as subtle as a shiver
Remember to be happy, he says,
tells me it's all that matters

I can hear the roar of the sea
and I know how much he longs to go there,
no place can comfort him like the beach

It's july, and the flowers outside the patio
are in full bloom,
magnolia, wild orchids, sunflowers

He always calls me his flower garden,
because I'm colorful and flourishing in the summer,
but withers and fade as soon as winter comes along

I wonder what will happen
when he's not there to water me
next year

Pour
your soul
into the cup
on my table
Then cover it
with boiling water

Pray for your answers
and hear the sighs
of relief
as the riddle
unravels

You know on the days
when your body is absolutely broken,
your mind in hysterical despair
and you feel as if
you cannot take this
any longer

Those are the days
when you are being tested,
when whatever you choose to believe in
is building your strength

For how can you know victory
if you haven't known defeat

I may not
be much for you
to look at
but at least
I'm pretty
inside

The clock ticks
Faster
Minutes pouring out
I'm leaking
Dreams never uttered
turns into dust
as they fall
I thought
that by now I'd be whole
but instead
I'm quickly dissolving

Beautiful things,
how easy they are to love,
compared to people

Those summer nights,
cigarettes and cheap champagne
I was a sparkling mess and you
were basking in my misery,
shamelessly
You kept the secrets I shared
for a while,
stored them like tiny butterflies
in a glass jar
But I should have known
that glass break,
intoxication wears off,
summer rarely lasts
Although I never expected
you to be the kind
who would triumphantly rise
out of other peoples ashes

His voice was different
Sounding like a song
written in a language I did not know
It scared me
Because he seemed happy
Will you lay down with me, he wondered
I instantly surrendered in his arms and said nothing
Only listened to his irregular heartbeat that once
made me feel safe
We must have dozed off for a while
because suddenly we were surrounded by blackness
in a cloud of heavy rain
I touched his lips and I knew he watched me in the shadows
Where is the sky you gave me, I asked
He laughed quietly
A beautiful, genuine laugh
It scared me
Because he seemed happy

There was a hypnotic sensation in the silence that followed
and we both knew that all the ecstasy of the night
would disappear in the first blush of the morning
Could we survive on our own
Without the cord that kept our secrets held together
Without our love that was so achingly rare
Did we even exist without each other
or were we mere memories scattered in silvery ashes
on the floor of a burnt down house

I still carry the smell of him on my hands
I wash them over and over,
he's still there,
constantly
As if his ghost imprint is glued to my palms,
my fingers, wrapped around my wrists,
seeping
out of my pores

He asks why i'm so lonely,
but I just turn my head, not wanting
to face him
I have no answer, I don't know
Forgiveness, I've begged for it
so many times it has become imprinted
on my tongue, stained my knees
I have failed in so many friendships,
lost so many lovers
and I don't know what I did wrong
Maybe, I'm blind
to my own wrongdoings
and I don't want to spoil him –
that's why I won't let him in

Come with me to the sea
Where all weight
is lifted
Let us swim to the far end
and disappear
Turn into pearls molded by movement
Imagine how comforting
to know that you become more valuable
by each layer
Instead of less

Who gave you the right,
to place the whole world on my shoulders
To fill my body with your waste,
rotten fruit,
to spit inside of me and then chain the lid

Who gave you the right,
to demolish the trust I had so carefully collected
To step with your dirty boots through my house,
leave stains all over me,
tear my walls down,
and strip me to the foundation

She was silk to his hands
but unreachable
Honey to his tongue
but also the drug that could kill him,
disable him, leave him
sick
with envy
She was cinnamon and spring flowers to his senses
Smells that made his heart soar and mouth water
But she was also thick smoke to his lungs
and sharp needles in his eyes
Pleasure and pain
All at once

A blood moon hangs low above me
Feverish dreams keep knocking me out
Suddenly I dive through the sky
into another dimension,
another life
He reach for me
and we dance under the crimson heaven until our feet ache
and our hearts open
A fire burn within me and he is my gasoline –
watering my thirst
Hold me, hold me forever
and he says *yes yes I will I will baby I will*
There goes a soothing breeze through me and I know he's real
As long as I keep dreaming

Light steps
turned weary
Clear eyes
shadowed with grief
A pale version
of what I used to be
staring back
through tainted windows
Who is she, that stranger
I wonder what happened
to the real me

I lay awake on my bedroom floor
watching the dancing shadows on my walls
The sun is about to set
and is blessing my room with a rose gold shimmer
At least there is some beauty
to the last hour of despair
I think about cities that I've visited
and cities that I'll never see,
what a tiny fraction I've seen of the world
A light breeze sneaks in through my open window
and it makes me long for freedom
What if I could leave my body here on the carpet
just for a brief moment,
and travel
with the wind
like a dandelion spirit

Can you still love me
when I am nothing,
when I have nothing
but myself

Close your eyes
I'm just going to
sprinkle
some glitter
over your face
Not that you aren't
pretty
already, but even
you
who make the life of others
sparkle
Needs taking care of
sometimes

The midnight air was filled with falling petals,
and under that rare rose moon I was born
Getting drunk on instrumental vibrations,
my voice interlaced with tunes of a piano unwanted,
abandoned by the stream of music that I aimlessly swam in
I turned into an immortal bird
drinking from the fountain of life,
radiant in my happiness
No longer imprisoned
in the empty words of childhood diary dreams,
no longer in chains of agony for not daring to live truthfully,
no longer a slave under my own minds made up limitations
Free to take off –
at last

Will you sing for me
when I don't remember how to use my voice
Will you dance for me
when I lose the ability to move my body
Will you tell me about the world
when I can no longer see
And, will you continue to love me
even when I forget
that I love you

Skin in full bloom,
streaks of river
flooding in the heat
You,
tracing the map of memories,
painted all over valleys,
chaotic crossroads,
beautiful deserts,
mysterious caves
Lost in the landscape
of my body,
unhurriedly finding your way
to its essence

You are all over me,
reside in every corner of my room
You are the trees guarding me in the woods,
towering over me in my garden

You are my shadow under every moon-lit sky,
moving through me like thick blood through veins
You are in the colorless evening landscape,
the swift breeze kissing my neck

You are in the warmth of the sun,
the coolness of water
You are the first snow,
coming down on me like a silky veil

You are my anchor,
in every stormy sea
You are the reason for everything
that I will ever be

The moon lay resting in my hands,
providing guidance as I quietly stumble
into the night
My wet, glittery skin is nothing
compared to her brilliance and for a moment
I forget
that I'm no longer whole,
that I've been divided in two pieces
One *before*, and one *after*
I whisper to her, my light in the dark,
that this is our secret,
that no one else must know
Because at least I want to be in one piece
to them, still a complete human being,
even though I'm broken in half

I do not
want to be
strong
anymore
I want to be
weak,
fall apart,
be carried
By you

During the night I call for you, *come back*
come back to me, please
The memory of you fades
just the way a breath does in winter,
and soon you'll be gone
You'll be a trapped soul in the trees,
a ghost wandering in endless circles, and I'll be free
I was offered a glimpse into the future,
a hint of what I would be without you,
a promise that I would master the machinery of living
on my own
Still I plead for your return
Come back, come back to me, please

I wash my eyes with gilded sand,
grains of a future unknown
My lips are burnt with words we never told each other,
like kisses for you to rediscover
I'm turning golden and I stand completely still,
maybe you'll notice me now
Those raspberry flavoured sweets you liked lay in my hands,
tempting you to come closer, to taste me,
to remember how luscious and lovely I could be

Eyes flutter,
A last twitch of my emptied body,
not a speck left of my soul
He folds me into origami and kiss me farewell,
bye litte bird, off you go
I crumble, like buildings falling,
metal against flesh, thunder to a fragile heart
Begging for forgiveness but he resists
I knew I could never be anyone's,
but his

Like broken lights
in deserted street corners,
I am constantly flickering
Wishing to attract your attention,
yearning for fixing
but bypassed

I'm crawling my way through the gravel
Followed by traces of blood
Ruby red,
like a tiny river in sunset hour
The birds sing beautifully,
calling on the angels to come pick me up
Take her home, it is time
Unexpectedly I'm floating,
light hair surrounding my face like a halo
The heart quiet,
my stained soul pure once again –
entirely at peace
On the ground below lay an empty shell,
crushed under the foot of a stranger

Peeling skin, onion layers of untruth
Salted caramel lips and served kisses on silver plates,
hidden under shadowed veils
Silky curls turning into melting butter in warm hands,
trembling breaths like footsteps in sand
An angel oak watching quietly,
saving memories among its heavy branches
Love untamed
Youth deflowered like sprouting seeds
Quick insignificant moments,
forever stored in the leftover piles
of burning embers

It's way past midnight,
most of the city lights
have gone out
The bar on the corner
has been put to sleep
and my street is empty
I think about
the people whom I saw
from my kitchen
window,
leaving the bar,
and pray that they got home
safely

I want to be happy
but everyone I care for
abandon me,
no matter how much of my love
I pour into them
Once their cup is full
I'm of no use
anymore
Unless they show up
for me to refill it

Thinking about the dream we created,
how it made living so simple
Out here, they're all lying about everything,
it drives me mad
My hands are tied,
all creativity melts into my tissue and disappear
No one is genuine anymore,
I smell the greed within them as they pass me,
it reeks all over the city

I'll help you, if you give me something back

If he doesn't look at you with a burning desire,
doesn't touch you like you're the softest of silk –
he's not the one

You left me, so easily
Brushed past me like I was transparent
or thin air
as if non of our memories mattered,
or even happened
It fascinates me,
how someone can love so deeply
and then forget,
quicker than a shallow breath

Sticky syrup
Tangled in my hair
A moth hovering above
Flickering lights
Making me spin around like a drunk
Cold concrete
Covered in crystal webs
Kissed by peculiarity
Still empty
Within

I am scared of not being seen
Still I don't want anyone to see me

A velvet dress
hangs in the sun rays by the window
Dark burgundy
made for a sinner
The room is empty
echoing silence and memories of voices
bouncing on the walls
A lock of golden hair lay curled in a corner
and the floor is covered with broken glass –
sparkling like silver teeth
The coffee table has been turned over
creating a marble wall
for protection
maybe
or turned out of rage
Big paintings of people with hollow faces
staring down between gilded frames
keeping secrets
of what happened there
when no one else was watching

I'll kill you, he said
If you ever leave me
How those words excited me
I was like a rabbit running towards bright headlights
Always drawn towards destruction
He thought I was desperately in love with him,
that I needed him
But I never needed anyone,
I was stronger on my own

We are the shadows
behind the bright stages
The quiet ones
in all the noise that surrounds us
We are the supporters among the people
who does everything to pull us down
The ones who carry all the weight on our shoulders
But to be all this
We silence our hearts and our souls
and the roaring talents we possess
In order to make others happy

The world
has in some way
humbled me
I used to be a frozen lake,
solid and cold
Now I'm a waterfall
in a tropical rain forest,
warm
and gently moving

If you feel
in this very moment
as if everything is falling
apart
As if you're turning into
a ghost
of your own self
Then let me tell you
that
I know how tired you are,
how you struggle
But I also know
what it's like to heal,
to mend the brokenness
within
and see colors
return once again
Sometimes,
it just takes a little
longer

Imagine your words
turning into permanent marks on your skin
Your prejudices
becoming your own reality

Would you act
differently?

Deep under layers of skin, flesh,
blood rushing – we're identical
Fragments of pasts, atoms in flight,
nothing but stillness, but we're also
everything in motion
How tragic it is,
that we make difference
of what we can see,
without paying attention to
what we can't

Dear moon, cluster of stars,
angels of the universe
Please, please guide me home
I am tired
of constantly moving forward
I am scattered
in so many places

Look for me
Where shadows lay along the sides of the river
Come find me
On an island set in a wild sea
Follow me
Down the winding paths of burning mountains
Then make love to me
Among the dancing sycamore trees

Kneeling on the floor, tears of amethyst
turning into a purple pool around him
I watch him silently for I feel nothing
There he is, so weak and weaping,
drowning in the mess he also once created
to drench my soul
I remember him holding me down
and his blank stare as I crumbled,
utterly empty of emotion
Beautiful and tragic all at once
He shook me until the truth fell out at his feet,
like broken glass figures crushed in anger

How deep we hurt each other, him and I,
and how much we still love,
unconditionally, when we are able

I found refuge
in my own solitude
saw the brilliance
of me
take off into a spiral flight
away over rooftops,
until it ceased to exist

I confused loneliness
with the preservation of
womanhood
Thought that a guarded
heart
was a strong one

For a while
I didn't love anyone,
nor did I wanted to be loved

How many times will I
have to apologize for my presence,
before I accept that I am
who I am for a reason

How often will I
have to continue to bang my head against dead ends,
before my written path reveal itself
in front of me

Rotten leaves
The smell of old dirt
Strangers, who might be lovers
Walking past each other
as if they were the last on earth
Ice cream
Melting in the hands of a crying child
Unseen by parents who are too occupied
to notice

Frances Ivy

Who are you,
beneath the layers of what you have been told you are
Who are you,
on the inside of your imaginary inside

He drops a handful of roses on the pavilion floor
Why did you leave, why why tell me,
God damn it
Everything shatters,
our dreams fade away into midnight
To see him there, so frail and so utterly devastated
completely takes me off guard
I didn't know he loved me that much
In my dusty pink dress
I'm as fragrant as the flowers he dropped,
as lush as a field of daisies –
still he can't see me, even though I'm right there

Beautiful moments, bypassed
Hotel pools once filled with laughter, now deserted
Sad children, overlooked
Sunny days missed behind curtains
Insecurities mistaken for arrogance
Fallen leaves on pavements, swept away as dirt
Clothes forgotten in the rain
Kids toys, run over by cars
Lovers, fighting
Families, breaking
Animals, hurting
Beggers, ignored
People who wish their life was different

– Things that bother me

I used to write about happy times,
as in having pink roses scattered all over me
or him kissing my body,
his eyes glimmering with content
The reality is that I wrote about something long gone,
hiding in vivid memories as the truth of who I was fell apart
For years I clawed on walls
trying to find that which I missed so dearly,
making sure no one really knew how much I suffered inside,
how many demons I was fighting
Constantly running,
further and further away from myself,
looking for happiness in other places –
in other people
When I look back at that time now
I realize
how much I was actually molded by those moments,
how important that was for my self growth
I look back at when I used to write about happy times,
knowing that in some ways I also wrote about the future

Entangled in a spider's web
Stuck in a sinkhole
Vulnerably praying before the altar –
I am filled to the brim
Anxious breath, delicate ribs
A ripple in the serene sea

How peculiar
to appear so poor
in the midst of prosperity

If he's the type playing games
Putting a heavy weariness on your heart,
leaving you feeling uneasy –
Then he's not good enough for you,
he's not yet enough of a man to love

All of us are flowers
Some strong and proud,
able to stand tall
through the most revengeful weather
Some delicate
like the wings of a butterfly,
pulverized by the softest touch
Some full of color,
bursting with luminosity
and some shy of their own complexion,
hiding behind their leaves

Untalented
Am I without
substance
Is there nothing
to me but
hopes, and wishes
An idea of myself
that doesn't
exist

It is a heavy burden
Trying to rule your kingdom
with soft hands
In a world so hardened

Do not let
hate
enter your precious
mind
Do not let
anger
overtake your
body

I will whisper to you
words of honey
I will make your soul blossom
even when winter falls around us
And I will carry your seeds
in my safest chamber

Words
keep pouring out
of me
Like a tap
with unlimited water

I hang my tears
on a string before you
where you're forced to look
It's right there now,
out in the open
for everyone to see

Look at what he's done to me

Loving you
was too complicated,
not a pretty story at all
I gave you everything
but you gobbled greedily
on every caring gesture I offered

So forget about me,
wipe your mind clean
I will not be there to feed you
any longer

Frances Ivy

In my hands
I carry a bunch
of sleeping souls
Tired and worn out
they come to me
So I give them a place
to rest

Back among favorite streets
Surrounded by buildings that saw me take my first step
into the world
I wear the pearls you gave me,
wrapped around my neck,
down my collarbones
The sky in its soft hues casting a pastel filter over sand colored
stone, giving the impression of a rose quartz dream
I've thought a lot about us lately,
how I always did my best to please you,
and how this city so mercilessly changed us –
Especially you
The sweetness of our naivety lingers in street corners,
the little blue bakery on your street, still the sugar coat of it all
How you kissed me in nights of insomnia,
made love to me under milky moons
You ripped me apart but you also healed me
Always since then, in som way present,
as a sliver of the past

Give me your pain,
all of your sorrows
Fold them neatly –
Then hand them over
I have suffered so much
already
I can take a little more

I wave goodbye to the sadness
and she floats away like a sailboat on a ghostly sea
Along with her goes the old anxiety
and the trembling fear,
hand in hand like two lovers
I stand on the shore watching them
move further away
like the three musketeers
off to fight another war
In a way I'd like to go with them,
because we've been allies
for such a long time
But I just stand there, empty but also so full
Scared of starting over but also free,
finally, to be perfectly happy

Beaten, stumbling,
scraping my knees
I ran
Away from this city,
away from him
It was the dirtiest scene
but there was nothing ugly
in it

One day,
so subtly,
the heaviness
started to lift
The fist
within my chest
weakened
and the clasp
around me
was released

Frances Ivy

Almost winter
But inside of me
summer is thriving

You walk
with your head
low
thinking that
no one understands
how you feel
But if only
you would lift your gaze
you'd see
that we all
hurt
in some way

In my dreams, I'm drowning
Slimy creatures grabbing my feet,
my legs, my arms – whispering pretty words in my ears –
You belong here, with us
The depth gives me a sense of ease and I,
who used to fear water,
suddenly embrace the emptiness
as it swallows me

An angels touch,
stroking my hair as I gasp for air,
choking by the thorns engraved in my throat
A swirl of color passes by and I remember thinking –
Is this what my life has looked like
Filled with movement and magic,
swift and unreachable,
one moment here
the next somewhere else
How come that I never noticed,
until now

18548256R00062

Printed in Poland
by Amazon Fulfillment
Poland Sp. z o.o., Wrocław